FROM THE
OUTSIDE
OF THE
FENCE

FROM THE
OUTSIDE
OF THE
FENCE

What The Public Doesn't Know And Should Know
About America's Corrupt Penal System

CLAIR BLOOM

FROM THE OUTSIDE OF THE FENCE
WHAT THE PUBLIC DOESN'T KNOW AND SHOULD KNOW
ABOUT AMERICA'S CORRUPT PENAL SYSTEM

iUniverse books may be ordered through booksellers or by contacting:

iUniverse
1663 Liberty Drive
Bloomington, IN 47403
www.iuniverse.com
1-800-Authors (1-800-288-4677)

Because of the dynamic nature of the Internet, any web addresses or links contained in this book may have changed since publication and may no longer be valid. The views expressed in this work are solely those of the author and do not necessarily reflect the views of the publisher, and the publisher hereby disclaims any responsibility for them.

Any people depicted in stock imagery provided by Getty Images are models, and such images are being used for illustrative purposes only. Certain stock imagery © Getty Images.

ISBN: 978-1-5320-9068-4 (sc)
ISBN: 978-1-5320-9069-1 (e)

Library of Congress Control Number: 2020904929

Print information available on the last page.

iUniverse rev. date: 03/12/2020

PRISON DEFINITION

The house that Satan builts

CONTENTS

INTRODUCTION

In *From the Outside of the Fence*, you'll learn just how the US prison system works and how corrupt it is from top to bottom. Everyone has their hands out.

This book is about the corruption in the Department of Correction, including for-profit private prisons, describing the cutback of food expenses to shoddy health care that leads to senseless deaths that no one takes responsibility for.

In the Texas Prison Bid'ness blog, it says, "Prison in a box—just unpack, assemble and fill with people. That's it in a nutshell!!" Read their blog. It's very interesting.

I've interviewed countless former inmates and their families, including many former prison guards. If you want the truth, go to the source.

I met a woman in a hospital waiting room as we were both waiting for our husbands while they had cancer surgery. We chatted for about five hours. After that first visit, we became good friends. I came to know a lot of her family history.

Barbara's is a sad story. She's had a lot of pain in her life. She has four children: two boys and two girls. Some of her tale saddened and angered me. After being friends for about a year, I asked if I could write her story. Barbara agreed with me, stating that the average person doesn't have a clue about the penal system.

We hear nonsense news stories about what Hollywood celebrities eat for breakfast, how much the celebrities make, and what their opinion is on everything from fruit to nuts. Who cares? There are more important and serious issues investigative reporters could delve into … and I mean deep issues. We could really get down to the root of corruption, not a fluff piece about who called who a name on Twitter.

I felt I had to tell Barbara's story because she could be any one of us. While researching the penal system, I found most of the information appalling, and that is an understatement. Many stories are downright criminal but not perpetrated by inmates. The perpetrators are the penal system and the employees who think they are above the law.

This is Barbara's story as told to me. I researched and wrote the rest.

CHAPTER 1

BARBARA AND THE VERDICT

It was a warm, balmy September evening. My husband was doing paperwork in his office. I was in the living room, reading one of my favorite authors, Chekhov. Life was good. All our children were doing well and had good jobs and nice families.

Then bang! Our lives changed in an instant when we received a conference call from the Superior Court sentencing trial of my inmate in Maryland. It was the first we had heard about it. The judge had questions he wanted my husband to answer. After he did so, the judge asked my husband if he wanted to listen in on the court proceedings, which my husband did.

My husband came into the living room to tell me who was on the line. "Do you also want to listen in?"

"No," I said, "I'll wait until it's over."

I went into our bedroom, closed the door, and prayed until the call was over. Twenty minutes later, the trial was over, and my husband called me into the living room. He told me to sit down. I couldn't move.

I said, "Tell me now." I could see the pain and agony on his helpless face.

The next thing I heard was a guttural cry, like a fatally wounded animal in the distance. The next thing I remember, I was crumpled on the floor. How long I lay there, I don't know. All I know is that I heard "eight years." Nothing else mattered. My heart

1

cracked, never to be mended. It was eight years for what should have been two and a half to three years, which I have since learned.

I walked around the house for weeks, not going out and not talking to anyone, not even my husband at times. He understood and was very patient with me. The tears and heartache wouldn't subside.

The feeling was like when a loved one dies and you can't accept it. You see that person everywhere you go. It was like when my mother died. Everywhere I went in Montana, I thought I saw her in a crowd or in a store. I would walk closer, just to realize it wasn't her. I'd walk away with tears streaming down my face. Was I irrational? Maybe yes. But at that moment, it was my mom. It was a way of holding on to her.

The same thing happened when my inmate was incarcerated. I would see a man from the back with the same build, hair color, and haircut, and I wanted to go over and hug him. Other times I would wait with tears in my eyes for a man to turn around so I could see my inmate's face. Sometimes I would call out my inmate's name, but no one turned around. Reality isn't all it's cracked up to be.

As the years go by, every holiday gets harder and harder. Depression sets in, and I want to stay in bed until after the new year. But I can't because I have a loving husband to think about, along with my other children and their families. I haven't put up a Christmas tree or decoration since that day in September, and I never will. My husband is very supportive, and I know he hurts as well. I purchase Christmas gifts for my inmate every year and put them in a large box, staying there until his release.

It must be that way somewhat for other mothers, fathers, and siblings—well, some siblings don't care either way—just wishing the years would fly by and our loved one would come home.

If you think incarceration can't happen in your family, think again. The color of your skin, the clothes you wear, and the state you live in can all count against you. I clung to my faith, but this time evil won. The arresting officer lied in court. (He used the old taillight-is-out scam). The DA lied. So sue me. You know who you are. I can just imagine a DA reading this book and asking, "Is she writing about me?" Yes, all of you.

As the years tick by slowly, your life on "the outside of the fence" is forever changed. You worry every single day and pray your inmate will survive the copious violence that is constantly occurring in the prison. Even in a minimum-security facility, you carry that burden until your inmate is released.

There is no shortage of hate in the prison system. I'm not looking for sympathy. These are the facts, period. Most people believe that they could never have a loved one serving time. Or so I thought. Adversity can affect anyone without political connections or a president who will pardon them. But those people special, not like the rest of us normal people.

While I was researching this book, I learned a lot about people. I wrote this book to clear up the misconception that all inmates are the scum of the earth, a misnomer at best. People make mistakes; others, I believe, are born evil. From the outside of the fence, you worry day in and day out about your loved one until he or she is released. And you pray that the inmate has an honest and helpful parole officer. If a mentally ill person gets sent to prison, no matter what degree of the illness, that individual has no chance in hell behind bars.

One worries about rape, gang rape, beatings, theft, someone planting illegal drugs in his or her area, or if there is a disturbance in a facility. We on the outside of the fence cannot get any information. General information from the news may not be correct. You call to see if your inmate is safe, and the phones may be shut off. Or you get an answer, "Everything is under control."

"Okay, but is *my* inmate safe?" you ask.

They say, "Can't answer that at this time."

So you wait not so patiently until your inmate can call you. Only then can you breathe normally.

The public is concerned that some prisons are too close to their neighborhoods. I would be more concerned with the people in the hood who aren't behind bars. Most prisons are out in nowhere land. You usually need a map and a compass to find a place.

The average citizen doesn't know—or doesn't want to know—what goes on behind the barbwire fence. "Lock them up and throw away the key" is all too often repeated. That doesn't apply to all inmates, like nonviolent offenders such as drunk drivers, marijuana smokers, thieves, and so on. These nonviolent acts can be rehabilitated. Instead of incarcerating them, place them somewhere to be rehabilitated and become productive citizens.

In this book, you will find answers to many of these questions and more about the whole corrupt penal system perpetrated by the so-called justice system. Justice for all? Not! Overcrowding the prisons is not an answer. It's more of a cause than a solution. What do you think a nonviolent offender learns in prison? The answer is what they shouldn't know and how to stay alive. Sure, there are incorrigibles, but we must not lump all inmates in one category. That's like saying that all persons who are not in prison are good, God-fearing people. Not! Take the priests who have abused children for centuries. (This I know firsthand because my father was in a Catholic orphanage and saw what the priest did to other boys. My father had an identical twin brother, and the priest didn't dare mess with them.) How about the four hundred child abusers who weren't prosecuted in one certain state? How about the politicians who break the law every day and so on?

CHAPTER 2

BARBARA AND LIVING WITH THE PAIN

I begged the Lord to take my life. I couldn't stand the pain or anticipate when it would end. All I could think of was eight wasted years. As it turned out, the years for my inmate weren't wasted. He got a college education, read the classics that he would have never read on the outside, took writing and several paralegal courses, and received a theological degree, to name just a few of his accomplishments. When released, my inmate will have two books published.

My husband and I were living in Montana at the time of his sentencing. We debated whether we should stay there or move to Maryland. In moving to Maryland, we would be able to visit our inmate eight days per month. But we would be living from one visit to the next for years. That's not the life we had envisioned when my husband retired. So we made the painful and difficult decision to stay put and give our inmate as much support as we could from where we were.

I write five to eight times a week, as my inmate's siblings do not visit. We fly to Maryland as often as we can afford. At our age, the visits take their toll on our health. My inmate's ex told me over the phone in an acrimonious voice that she hoped my inmate would get life! As if eight years for a victimless crime that she knew about and had a hand in wasn't enough. I think the ex feared that everyone would find out her involvement in the incident. The ex was aware of what was going on and was an accomplice at one point.

A week before we flew to Maryland for the last appeal, I had a dream. I saw my inmate walk up to the side of my bed, touch my arm to wake me up, and say, "Mom, I'm not getting out early." And my inmate walked slowly away. I woke up sobbing. I didn't tell anyone about my dream at the time. I wrote the dream in my diary and showed it to my husband when we arrived home. We went to court, and my inmate was right. He was denied an early out.

Don't get me wrong. My inmate committed a victimless crime and should pay for it, but eight years when others received two to three years? What I'm saying is that there is no consistency in the judicial system. Yes, they say they have guidelines, but I also know that the judges have the discretion to do what they think is right. Otherwise, why would a rapist receive three years in prison? It's ridiculous.

The deals are made before the inmate even enters the courtroom, all among the judge, DA, and court-appointed lawyer, who incidentally are as useless as a sneaker full of shit. Why would a court-appointed lawyer bother to look at the facts and discrepancies and then interview witnesses when he or she gets paid next to nothing? What is the incentive for a court-appointed lawyer to do the right thing and the best job he or she can do for an inmate? Oh please! The guilty sentence is all packaged and wrapped in a big black bow before anyone enters the courtroom.

One witness was a police officer who was with her partner. She had told my inmate that if he needed a witness, he could contact her. But they used the other police officer for the witness, the one who used the illegal stop and search. The court-appointed lawyer didn't ask any questions or cross-examine the witness. The court-appointed lawyer could have asked why the prosecutor didn't have the inmate's statement at hand in the courtroom. She could have gotten off her hands and asked questions.

The prosecutor told the judge that he always writes up the charges and statements made by each defendant on every case he prosecutes. He told the judge that he could not find them in this case. The judge should have recessed the court so the absentminded prosecutor could have gone back to his office to find them. After all, his office was in the courthouse. At this time, all charges were his word against the defendant. Who wins that round? Again, that's a rhetorical question. The shit-poor prosecutor didn't have his ducks in a row or was too lazy. Or it was both. He was a big shot in a small hick town.

It's been years now, and I still worry every day for my inmate's life. All of us who have inmates should be concerned. We have a legitimate reason to be anxious. Some inmates have a short time left on their sentences and never get released alive.

On May 3 at 6:36 p.m. in my inmate's prison building, an officer planted a cell phone in my inmate's shoe, which was inside his bunk area. My inmate spotted it when he returned from work duty. He then complained.

The officer said, "Put that in your book!"

So I am. You know who you are. Then he said he was just kidding. My inmate could have received five extra years for "just kidding." Why would an inmate deliberately leave a cell phone for all to see in a shoe while on work duty? Where did the officer get the cell phone? They are not allowed in this prison.

My inmate had witnesses to the whole affair, and they agreed to testify if my inmate wanted to pursue the infringement. There's more corruption and harassment in another chapter.

Another inmate tried to molest my inmate in the shower. The offender picked on the wrong person. Why are there no officers guarding the shower areas? That's where most of the offenses occur, out of sight. My nerves are shot worrying if my inmate will one day walk or be carried out of prison. Many don't get that opportunity to walk out.

Another road my inmate will have to travel upon release is adjusting to clean air, freedom, and humanity. He must find a job. Most employers won't hire an ex-felon, not even nonviolent ones. Finding a place to live has the same challenge.

My husband and I are on this journey with our inmate. We won't find peace until this nightmare is over. The sentences are not for the inmates alone; the families serve right along with them. We all live our hell from outside the fence. We live in another state, but our inmate lives in another world. I pray every night that Jesus will keep my inmate safe. I worry every day that someone else may plant contraband in his area or poison his food. I worry that he might be gang-attacked or catch HIV.

It's a dog-eat-dog world every day. Even if you mind your own business, someone or other won't let you. Other inmates provoke, saying things like, "You think you're better than us. You'll be back." The guards are not any better, saying the same things, taunting and demeaning the inmates. If you don't have a clear picture of who you are, you will start thinking you are worthless. Years of hearing all the negatives is like a captive being brainwashed.

I haven't slept much at night all these years. If I make it through these eight years without having a stroke or fatal illness, I'll be surprised. Stress is a killer.

Every Day I Cry

Every day I cry for the years we've missed and the hugs we've lost. My heart breaks for all those years without you, your smile, your laugh, and your jokes. I know nothing will ever be the same. No more Santa, a.k.a. George Washington. No more watching the same movie over and over again with you knowing all the dialogue. I remember the dozen times we sat through *Star Wars* and how much you loved that movie. How about the time I brought cookies to the movies for you and me that tasted like roach spray? You and I gagged and laughed at the same time.

The sun will shine again for me when my angel flies free. Without you, I'm reminded every day how precious life is. I can see the sun come up early in the morning and how the rain smells, especially in the spring, but you can't.

I think of you alone even though there are people and noise all around you. You write feverishly, trying to distance yourself from the insanity. You are my inspiration to let people know how unjust are the just and how corrupt are the corruptible.

One day we will walk the streets of Europe and reminisce about the time years ago when we did just that. Those will be good times. Every day I cry.

—Barbara

# CHAPTER 3

DEAD SOUL

I tried to read. It hurt to write. I was too wired to read or sleep. There are long days and nightmare nights. It's all false promises they don't keep. The walls close in around me, all cold steel and concrete. The light and life are taken away from me.

At night I read and cry. I cry as I write. I write as I die inside. Life is pulled from me. I need a soul to make me whole. I won't recover, as each day in here I get old. My mind just quits. Instinct takes over as each day grows longer. I'm getting hard-hearted, never to return. In hell I burn; on earth I mourn.

The warden is disinterested, concerned only about the appearances instead of the reality of life in prison. The warden leaves at 4:00 p.m. and arrives at 10:00 a.m.

People I hate hold me in place. I'm helpless to fight back, fearing extra years. I'm held in anger and darkness, a living hell. I remember the night before my incarceration, the last evening of living. My spirit is the last to go.

This place is designed to take the heart and hope away and replace it with hate and hopelessness. It is the Department of Corruption, DOC. There is no correction or rehabilitation.

Inmate 2989969 11, 30, 2013

Barbara's inmate, Carl B.

Inmate 2989969

Carl B.

CHAPTER 4

VICE, LEGAL AND NOT

When you think of the word *vice*, what comes up in your mind? Do you think of murder, any drug use, or larceny? Here are some vices people never think about.

First, I have to say that the opioid manufacturers should all go to prison because they knew the damage the drugs could do. They're addictive. Just because they're prescriptions doesn't mean they're good for you. The makers and doctors knew how addictive these drugs are. People think only strong drugs like opioids and cocaine kill. They do, but other drugs out there also kill.

Alcohol kills. College kids all over the country have died after drinking too much alcohol at frat parties. They use kitchen funnels to guzzle it. Has anyone not met an alcoholic? It's still one of the best sellers though. Prohibition didn't work. It fueled the Mafia. Well, to be fair it did give the Feds a job. Moonshine comes in this category. It also killed people because of the chemicals and dirty conditions that it was made in, such as car radiators.

Cigarettes surely kill. Look at what's in them. Formaldehyde is used in engineered wood products and also embalming fluids. Acetone and ammonia are used as cleaning products. Benzene is made from coal and crude oil. Arsenic is used to kill rats. Tell me that's not criminal. Why aren't cigarettes banned? Because they're a huge contributor to politicians.

It takes 240 joints to overdose on marijuana. Who's going to smoke that many in one day? If we regulate marijuana, our government will make billions in revenue. Instead we chose to put the casual smoker in prison. Look at the lives that would be saved if marijuana were legal at the federal government level and all in states. I'm not a smoker of any kind—and I don't advocate smoking of any kind—but to say marijuana kills is just foolish, unless you have an unscrupulous dealer who mixes other chemicals in a joint. Legalizing it would stop that practice.

Now the big-ticket item is guns. Guns kill. No, they don't, as the saying goes. But one has to wonder why a game hunter needs a semiautomatic or a high-powered scope to hunt deer, birds, or whatever they hunt. Do you think that's overkill? That's rhetorical. Why aren't automatic and semiautomatic guns and scopes outlawed? Big NRA contributions are why.

I'm not saying that everyone in the United States should give up their guns. One way or another, only the killers would have them. I believe guns are practical for self-protection and home safety, but to use a semiautomatic on an intruder is overkill. If we take away guns, killers will use knives, as we have seen in the news lately.

It amazes me that as far back as 1697, opium was being shipped to England from the Muslim world through the Arabian Sea. Think of the thousands of years that opioids were used. I don't think opioids will ever go away. As long as there is poverty, opium will continue to grow in the Middle East and Africa. I'm not putting marijuana in the same category. I just thought this fact was interesting and enlightening.

Prohibition

From 1920 to 1933, Prohibition couldn't control the sale and use of alcohol in the United States. Prohibition did more harm than good. It spurred the Mafia, murders, bootlegging, and speakeasies. And don't forget dirty cops.

Prohibition cost the US government $11 billion in lost tax revenue. It cost $300 million to enforce the law. Thousands of Americans died every year during that time because of tainted bootleg liquor. Hundreds of thousands were made criminals for possessing alcohol. Prohibition was meant to curb alcohol abuse. Instead people drank more, not less.

The only people making real money from marijuana are the cartels, not small dealers. Just look at the confiscated submarines, helicopters, boats, and firearms they have. The DEA and Border Patrol are no match for them. Why not hit the cartels where it hurts, in their pockets? Why not let our government legalize marijuana for federal taxes?

Prohibition didn't work in the 1920s, and it's not working with marijuana. Reagan's law did nothing to curb marijuana from coming into the United States. It only separated families and caused more crime.

As of 2017, eight states and Washington, DC, had legalized recreational marijuana. Medical marijuana is legal in twenty-eight states. Our government is behind the curve as usual.

CHAPTER 5

BARBARA RUN AMUCK

Department of Correction, now that's an oxymoron if I ever heard one. There is no correction. The system from east to west is out of control. The bottom line is to make money. Corruption is rampant from the judges down to the lowly correction officers. There's no greater offense for an inmate in the system who wants to try to excel. Courage is what it takes to stand up for oneself and speak one's mind. If an inmate wants to improve herself or himself, inmates and guards alike ridicule the inmate.

The ESPC website is deceiving at best. On one visitation room wall, a slogan reads, "Rehabilitation, success for life. Believe it or not, we care." That saying is for the visitors, not the inmates. The sign reminds me of those over the concentration camp entrance gates in Europe, "Hard work will set you free." Did it?

I cannot believe all officers and guards go to an academy, especially in a private prison where there seems to be no rules or consistency. They run for profit only, the bottom line. The administration does what it wants. Many prison guards are hired right off the street or from a McDonald's across from the prison. McDonald's is like a waiting station. Now if that doesn't give someone an ego, nothing does.

If guards or officers do go to a training academmcy, most are out to lunch while class is in session. I think all who work in the penal system should take psychology training. The requirements for a public prison are 200 hours of training at the facility. That's 120 hours within sixty days of obtaining the job. So basically it's on-the-job training.

Only a high school diploma or GED is required. Some DOC websites say training is generally required. There's no consistency. So a bully with a chip on his shoulder can get a correctional job. And I've seen plenty of chips. Anyone can put a chip aside to get hired. Power corrupts; absolute power corrupts absolutely.

Here's more from my favorite politician: "Attitude is a little thing that makes a big difference. Success is not final; failure is not fatal. It is the courage to continue that counts. If you're going through hell, keep going. So change your attitude and change your outcome!"

German concentration camp

The DOC websites sound good. They are designed to reassure the families, period. What goes on in the prisons is a whole other ball of wax. When families call the DOC with a complaint, they get a formulaic answer, "We'll look into it." Nothing is corrected; nothing changes.

Phone rates to call or receive calls from inmates are highway robbery. The Federal Communications Commission wanted to cap phone rates. But it was a no-go. The losers are the inmates and their families. Big money talks.

It is critical for inmates to receive rehabilitation before their release into society. But there is no incentive to have rehabilitation in some prisons because prisons prefer mass incarceration. It's a big business. Upon release, guards tell the inmates, "We'll see you back in a month."

Nonviolent offenders should be rehabilitated instead of serving prison time. Doesn't anyone think that a young offender will learn the art of crime in Prison 101? They will learn much worse than the offense that put them in.

According to the Vera Institute of Justice, one way of slowing down the recidivism rate is through education. 40 percent of inmates lack a high school education. Too many times there is no education in a facility. If there a chance for education, many inmates are sabotaged as the staff or mail room lose the school material. When I say *lose*, I mean throw away, not misplace. When the mail tracking number says the material arrived at the facility on a certain date and time and the inmate did not receive it, it was sabotaged, plain and simple!

Now ask yourself: Who pays for the lost school material? The answer is not the prison or school. The school charges to resend the material a second time. The family pays. The for-profit prison officials don't want inmates to get educated because there is a chance the offender won't return. Barbara has lost a lot of money because of these shenanigans.

If the inmate's families want to pay for their education, why not let them? There's no skin off the system's noses. Barbara has paid for courses, and in the middle of the program, the penal system takes that particular school off the table, and the course is never finished. Why? That's rhetorical.

A thirty-year study shows that 43 percent of inmates had access to literature, and this decreased the return of inmates. Some states have made it difficult for inmates in certain prisons to receive books. Why not encourage inmates to read and learn? Reading is an easy out, a time-out, if you will, from the chaos, noise, and din of prison. Reading takes you outside of your present world. It has a calming effect. Reading is learning, even if it's fiction.

This is a world of inconsistencies, oxymorons, half truths, whole lies, narcissists, and the "me" syndrome. In this world, we say "the hell with tomorrow" and live for the moment. We see it every day on TV. What are our youths supposed to think when they watch so-called reality shows with backstabbing, yelling, double-crossing, and physical fighting? Adults know these shows aren't real; children, on the other hand, absorb these shows like sponges. There is even violence in cartoons. It's no wonder kids don't have much respect for anything or anyone anymore.

There are approximately 3.5 million inmates in America. In 2010 more than 52 percent of the arrests were for marijuana. Nonviolent crime is the key term here. 88 percent of those were just for possessing marijuana. If the states were to release every nonviolent offender who was incarcerated for marijuana, the states would lose big money. Less prison business is less money for the states.

Let us examine the business of nonviolent crime. Empty beds mean no large profits for investors. Commissary and vending machine companies lose money. Companies that supply prisons charge outrageous prices. The prison system is a cash cow for the corporations that supply them. Here are just a few of the companies that make billions from the incarcerated with little or no oversight.

Eighty percent of phone calls go through one company. People can be charged exorbitant phone prices to talk to an inmate and also to open and close the phone service. A hedge fund owns one health-care provider for the prison system. One company had a $145 million contract to provide food for eight hundred prisons before maggots were found in the food. They have since been let go.

Barbara's inmate has talent and doesn't let anyone discourage or denigrate his talent. The one bright spot for Barbara's inmate is Pastor A. He has been very encouraging and helpful. She is very grateful for him. On the other hand, Pastor B is very surly to the inmates. He has voiced his opinion that the inmates are meant to endure all the crap they get. There's no compassion from a man of the cloth or respect for his position. Why does a man have a need to belittle others when they are close to falling themselves? Calling out "hey you" to an inmate denotes a ring of condemnation. Pastor B is in the wrong business. With that attitude, he should be a guard. He should ask himself every day, "What would Jesus do?" When judgment day comes around, he'll have to answer for the lack of compassion for his fellow man. And whether he thinks it or not, the inmates are part of his fellow man!

There is a beautiful mural in a prison visiting room. I stare at it intently each time I visit. It looks like a professional painted it, but an inmate did. It's amazing. On special occasions, I have received cards and craft gifts from my inmate that other inmates made. I cherish them all. These inmates have so much talent, and it's going to waste. They are truly artists, and I believe they could make a living from their craft.

The inmates in prison are treated and perceived to be lower than animals. It reminds me of the view that Hitler had for the Jews. Harass, harass, and harass, day in and day out, night and day, for no good reason except the guards can. I imagine it makes them feel superior.

True Story

Many years ago a company made up a psychology test using volunteer students. Half of the students were acting as victims; the other half were prison guards. The test was to denote that everyone is basically good. (Has no one ever heard of Hitler, Ted Bundy, or Jeffery Dahmer? And very few have ever heard of someone from 1893, Henry Holmes.)

I've heard it said that everyone has some good in them. I don't believe that for one minute. Have you ever looked into someone's eyes and seen emptiness? I have. If the eyes are the windows to the soul, then some people have no souls.

As the weeks went by, more and more student guards grew violent and began abusing their fellow students—beating, slapping, kicking, and punching them. At the end of the experiment, the result was that power corrupts!

Too much time behind bars is meant to break the soul and spirit, not build up confidence, since lack of confidence in themselves usually got the inmates in prison in the first place. If an inmate doesn't have faith, he or she may succumb to bad habits worse than what he or she was sentenced for. Long incarceration makes an inmate learn distrust and, worse, hate. The inmate also learns to lie and practice deceit.

Long-term inmates are more often lost in society upon release. They must learn to give up the hate, and some never do. Ex-felons have to try very hard to prove themselves. Many people will never trust an ex-felon. Who will hire an ex-felon? Very few. They are in a catch-22.

One cannot use the word *riot* when writing to an inmate, as in "Where were you when the riot started? Was it your block? Are you okay?"

It finally came out that the riot was not in my inmate's wing and that he was safe. My inmate was called into the warden's office for those sentences I wrote, as harmless as I thought they were. I am very far away from my inmate. I was very worried. My inmate explained to the warden that I didn't get much news where I lived. Thank God the warden understood my concern and my words weren't intended to be malicious. My inmate didn't get a mark or end up reported.

Other no-no words are *business, fights, gang, security, hidden, back road, transportation,* and *strike*. I can just imagine whole sentences blacked out, like letters from WW2.

America has run amuck, and its citizens don't care. The definition of *run amuck* is "an uncontrolled state" or "a violent turn." Or it means "without self-control." Since 2017, America has gone beyond running amuck. God bless America.

CHAPTER 6

BARBARA'S VISITATION

It was a cold, early morning. I was wearing only a skirt, blouse, and spring blazer for my first time visiting a prison. I was freezing, and my teeth were chattering as I waited my turn to go past the barbwire fence with a friend and enter the processing building. I never realized that it would be so cold this time of year.

It didn't take long for ignorance to show its face. My friend and I had finally found the prison. We parked the vehicle and stood with all the other visitors waiting to go inside by the first entrance gate. I had never been outside or inside a prison. I did not know what to expect at the first visit to see my inmate in a Maryland prison. I was green.

We were all chatting by the gate. The old pros were giving my friend and I pointers. All at once, we heard a shout, "Hey you!"

We all wondered whom he was referring to. Over at the second fence was a guardhouse. We heard someone yell "hey you" again from the guardhouse. Since my name isn't "Hey You," I paid him no mind. Nor did anyone else. We all asked ourselves, "Who is he talking to?"

I finally looked up toward the guard hut and heard with acrimony, "Yes, you!"

I've been called many things in my life, but "Hey You" was a first. I thought to myself, *What the hell did I do? I'm just standing here.*

I pointed to myself, and he yelled rudely, "Yes, take that jacket off."

I asked the women standing by me, "Why?"

They all said, "He thinks the color is tan." It was gray.

The woman told me to turn the jacket inside out where the lining was white with gray polka dots. What a putz! You can't learn ignorance. Either you're ignorant or you aren't. I suspect he always was. He was too lazy to come to the fence to talk to me and explain in a civil voice. After all, he had the gun. I certainly did not make any threatening moves.

A very kind woman gave me her warm jacket to wear until we were called into the reception area. I put it on over my own jacket. I am ever grateful to that generous lady. I had looked up the general rules for visitation before I had left home: no short skirts, no collarbone showing, only one ring, one pair of earrings, and thirty dollars in quarters in a see-through baggy. Nothing was said about the color gray.

Why do the guards feel a need to humiliate and dehumanize even the families? One doesn't want to complain in case they take it out on your inmate. Their vocabulary is very limited. The only words they know are "shut the fuck up."

There is a protocol to getting in line at the second gate. The person to arrive first places her thirty-dollar plastic bag on the ground by the gate; the second person places her baggy behind the first, and so on. It's clearly understood without a word spoken how it works.

It was finally our turn to enter the prison and give our ID and inmate's number. After a 105-minute wait in the cold, we were told my inmate was moved the day before to another facility. I gave the kind lady her jacket and told her what had happened.

The women were all sad for us. My friend and I returned to our vehicle and reached the other prison for a hour-long visit. I told my inmate, "Come hell or high water, I am going to find you."

My inmate said, "I know, Mom."

There was no problem with the color of my jacket at the new facility. Go figure! We spent the next day with my inmate for the full four hours. Don't give up on your children for a mistake they pay dearly for. A commercial on our TV asks, "What is freedom?" Think about it. We all take it for granted until it's taken away.

According to the ASPC website, one cannot wear orange to visitation. I can understand that. I have since given away all my orange clothes to prevent me from making a mistake and packing an orange piece of clothing. One cannot wear dark brown or a color that security staff wears. How the hell did I know what the security staff wears?

There's also no khaki, tan, or light brown. That about 100 percent of my husband's wardrobe. It's a good thing he wasn't with us. Dark brown pants and a tan, lightly printed shirt is what he normally wears. He might have been shot. They shoot anything that moves nowadays. Just for visitation, I have since purchased my husband a pair of checked, multicolored (blue, red, and green) golf pants with a bright yellow shirt. He stands out like a sore thumb, but he won't be confused as a guard. It works.

It must be mandatory to treat the visitors like prisoners (that is, rudely). Okay, our inmate made a mistake, but don't take it out on us. We are law-abiding citizens, and our inmate did come from a good and loving home. And no, I don't have anything up my ass. Can we go in now?

On another visit, my friend and I went through the scanner, and the buzzer went off.

The guard asked, "Do you have an underwire bra on?"

"Yes, I do."

She told us to go into the bathroom in the same waiting area and remove the wire. She said we couldn't just take the bra off. We could not go into visit without a bra on. I can understand that as well.

My friend also had an underwire bra on. We both trotted to the bathroom, took off our bras, and started chewing on the end of the bras to release the wire. After an agonizing fifteen minutes, my friend's wires came out. My bra was not cooperating. I kept chewing.

My friend had several layers of clothes on, including a sports bra over her regular bra. She said, "Take my bra, and I'll be okay with my sports bra."

The whole time we were in the bathroom, we were laughing with tears in our eyes at the absurdity of what we were doing. Someone knocked on the bathroom door, which made us laugh even more. So I put my friend's bra on, threw my new bra in the trash bin, and walked out with dignity. We had to laugh, or we would have cried at the time we wasted before the visitation. Ah, good times! Not! Remember, I came a long way to spend as much time as I could with my inmate. Again, we said nothing to him.

Another time my friend and I visited, all went well at check-in. We had a nice visit, as we always do. We had a few laughs and a trip down memory lane. We were looking forward to the future. We left the facility, and halfway home, we stopped at a coffee shop. It was a spooky, creepy little town with hardly anyone on the road or the street. We figured we'd be home in an hour or so. It was not to be.

We got our coffee and went to the vehicle, but it was a no-go. It wouldn't start. Now we were worried. It was almost dusk, and after trying to start it several times, it was obvious we were in trouble. Men were going in and out of the convenience store and paid us no mind. We gave up. We asked the store employee if there was a repair shop in town.

"Yes, across the street, but it's closed."

There were no hotels in the area and no cavaliers in that town. There were only tobacco-chewing shit-kickers. So we finally called AAA and were told it would take an hour and fifteen minutes to arrive. By now several men were lingering around the corner of the store, peering at us. Barbara and I were tired and a bit hungry, but we stayed locked in the vehicle until the tow truck showed up.

We were so relieved until he said he only had room in the cab for one of us. The other one would have to ride in our vehicle on top of the tow truck. I didn't think that was legal, but neither one of us wanted to be in the cab with a stranger. So we both got back in our vehicle, and the tow driver hoisted us up. It felt weird and not a little unsafe. We must have looked quite a sight, two women in a vehicle on top of a tow truck. The drivers passing must have asked themselves if they were seeing things. They all had strange expressions on their faces.

After a while, we decided to have a little fun with our predicament and wave at all the traffic going by. We were like a sideshow. Like I say, "You laugh, or you cry."

We were almost in the city when we heard a loud noise. We thought a chain had gotten loose. We looked behind us, and the whole back window of our vehicle was shattered. It was in place, but completely shattered. What next?

We finally arrived home, and the tow truck driver let us down with half the neighborhood looking on. We exited the vehicle. It was such relief! We were $275 poorer but in one piece. The tow truck company did not take responsibility for the broken window. Of course they didn't!

Once, I was visiting our inmate with my husband. I had black pants on; my husband had his clown pants on.

The security person said, "Your pants are too tight. Pull your pant leg up."

I said, "These aren't stretch pants."

She let me through the scanner without any buzzing. We got into the visiting room and saw two young ladies in tight jeans, and when they bent over, one could see their cracks. They made my pants look positively baggy. Go figure!

Another time when my husband and I visited, my wedding ring triggered the buzzer. It had never happened before. I have a very hard time getting it off because it's so tight. The guard told me to take it off. I asked if I could just put my hand through the scanner.

"No. Your whole body has to go through."

I went into the bathroom and put my hand under cold, soapy water. After a struggle, my ring finally came off. The guard told me to put my ring on the counter before going through the scanner. I told my husband who was behind me to keep his eyes on it. I could just hear the guard say, "I didn't see the ring!"

On another visit, my husband and I took off our shoes as usual to have them checked along with our coats. The staff checks those items by hand. I put my boots back on and went through the scanner, and it buzzed. I had to remove my boots again and go through the scanner once more. I was told to stand with my arms out while the female guard used a security wand and patted me down. There was nothing.

I asked if she were going to buy me dinner or at least a cigarette for that level of intimacy. I got a smile out of her. But I was written up and had to sign a paper. I don't know what the reason was because I didn't have my reading glasses and I can't see to read without them. Why complain and waste precious visiting time on a pair of boots? It was better than not seeing my inmate. I never told my inmate about this either. I don't expect the security crew to invite us in with open arms, but a little civility would be appreciated.

The time my inmate was brought to jail to wait for his court appeal, my husband and I had a noncontact visit, one where you talk into a dirty, encrusted phone with a glass partition between you and your inmate. We could visit in two-hour increments with an hour free in between. We did this for two days before the appeal date. A group of inmates was milling around the phones or waiting for a visitor.

When our two-hour visit was up, I said to my inmate, "We'll be back. Don't go anywhere."

My inmate cracked up and asked, "Mom, where would I go?"

I said, "Oh yeah!"

We all started laughing. The sergeant at the desk at this particular facility was very kind. We had a normal human-being conversation with him. We came back after an hour to complete our four-hours-a-day visit. That was the only visit in all the years of visitation that we did not have a guard make us feel like prisoners ourselves. I truly thank him for that.

When we visit, we are happy and sad at the same time. We have always laughed and joked together through thick and thin. We talk about the trips we've been through together and the good times, all positive. Yet with all the humiliation and inhumanity, the poison food, endless noise, and deaths in prison, my inmate manages to keep his sense of humor. The system hasn't taken that away from him.

Don't get me wrong. We are all sad inside, but we try to bolster each other up. I know after each of our visits, my inmate is quiet for a few days. He turns inward because he knows he won't see us for months or a year. I go to the airport crying every time. If I live long enough, we'll have more good times and trips when my inmate is released.

Joke (by Inmate Carl B.)

A guard asks an inmate, "Would you like nice cup of freedom?"

The inmate says, "I would love one. Thank you."

The guard replies, "Oh no! We can't have that. How about a cup of shut the fuck up?"

The inmate answers, "No thanks, I already had one."

 CHAPTER 7

REDUCING RECIDIVISM (REPEAT OFFENDERS)

According to the Vera Institute of Justice, one way to reduce recidivism is to educate an inmate. According to a blog, both Portugal and Sweden are closing many prisons. The Dutch have closed nineteen prisons since 2017. What is their success? These countries don't depend on politics to determine the rules. They use professional behavioral specialists, such as psychiatrists. Crime is low in Holland because of the relaxed marijuana laws and rehabilitation over punishment. It sounds perfectly rational to me. Some other countries with rehabilitating programs are Italy, Slovenia, Uruguay, Poland, and Ethiopia.

Why is a country like the United States so backward? Because of big money and lots of it. In Amsterdam, marijuana seeds are sold in flea markets out in the open and in cafés and food stores in brownie or candy form. It's not exactly legal, but as long as it's kept under control, the law looks away. I have visited Amsterdam several times before 2017 and never saw a problem on the street from marijuana.

St. Johnsbury Vermont Community Justice Centers are using support groups to help reduce recidivism. All states should follow suit. Researchers have found that cognitive treatment can reduce recidivism 25 to 35 percent, which means saving taxpayers money. It also means safer communities. So why isn't the program used more often in this country? It again comes down to money and beds filled. Most inmates are nonviolent.

They are not a public threat. Most are incarcerated for marijuana, theft (I don't mean grand theft auto as a business), and drunk driving.

Our archaic laws are making billions, thanks in part to crooked politicians. Are there any honest politicians? We all know that answer. So keep reading and educate yourself. Nothing is ever what we think it is. A. Ellis once said, "If a politician isn't born a liar, he will learn to become one."

Update 2019: The Netherlands

The country has apparently turned on its axis. The former peace-loving country has turned an important corner and joined the United States in its high crime rate from cocaine, not marijuana. Moroccan drug gangs have taken over this lovely country to distribute cocaine and ecstasy to all over Europe. The Netherlands government doesn't want to pursue them more vigorously because they don't want to be known for ethnic profiling. Really? Don't you think political correctness will be the death of all civilized countries? What a shame.

A flea market sign in Holland

CHAPTER 8

DOG CHOW

Not in the Four Food Groups

Okay, this has to be said: the chow served in most prisons wouldn't be classified as food, not even for dogs, as we will see in this chapter. There are three meals per day, two on Sunday. The coffee and juice are both watered down. One spoon of vegetables is so thoroughly boiled down that there are no vitamin or nutritional values left. You might as well drink the vegetable water.

What's on the menu today? Toenail stew, hair patties, yesterday's goulash with spit to round it off, runny pudding, or one tablespoon of canned fruit cocktail for dessert. There have been known feces matter, hair, and boogers in prison food. You think I'm kidding? Ask anyone who's been incarcerated.

No one incarcerated expects gourmet food, but one expects the food to be clean and obstacle-free. Who supervises the kitchen? Would you eat the food? Never mind. It's rhetorical. No wonder the guards bring in their own lunch bags.

One day, a guard, I guess he was bored or apathetic, sprayed mace in the cakes. He thought it was funny, I guess. Half the ward got sick. Was the guard reprimanded? I doubt it.

One day an inmate was eating what the prison called Salisbury steak. To quote an inmate, "They wouldn't know a Salisbury steak if Mr. Salisbury himself came galloping up on his horse." It's a hamburger patty, people. When the inmate couldn't chew the meat, he pulled a dreadlock out of his mouth. Do you want fries with that?

For those of you who aren't familiar with dreadlocks, they are pieces of hair strands matted together. It's an easy way not to have to worry about combing or washing one's hair. If you found one hair in your food, never mind a dreadlock, at a restaurant, you'd probably sue. Inmates have no recourse. In prison, chow is a whole other meatball. Prison food doesn't have to be five star, but it should be edible. Bon appetit!

That brings me to the prison commissary. When an inmate has no family or friends to ask for financial help or if he or she is indigent, the inmate has no choice but to eat the slop. Sorry, but I never met an inmate released from prison exclaiming, "Wow, the prison served great food." If an inmate has money in a commissary account, he or she can purchase food and other essentials. The money is deducted from the inmate's account, and the inmate receives the food one to two days later.

Say an inmate orders food from the commissary in the morning and gets transferred in the afternoon of the same day, always without notice of course. The inmate has five minutes to gather his or her things. Does the food order get rerouted or the inmate reimbursed? Hell no! It's the same old story. No one knows anything about the order. Food and money get lost in the system. By now, you know what I mean when I say "lost." I'm just telling it like it is. It happens all the time, no matter the prison. If you complain to the DOC, you get the stock answer, "I'll look into it." That must be a recording. DOC should just be honest and say, "Kiss your money goodbye."

I did hear about one inquiry to the DOC as to where one inmate's order was. The DOC said, "I saw the order on the truck," the same vehicle this inmate was traveling on. It was doubtful the order was on that truck. Did the truck make a drop-off stop? Was the truck hijacked?

The same thing happened to another inmate who was also transferred to another facility. The box with his lowly possessions arrived but was a little light. His TV, new socks, shoes, music, and CD player were missing. I can imagine shoes and socks walking away, but a TV? I think not! There should be a tracking system on food orders and possessions. I believe there is. If the facility tracked the food orders and possessions like they do inmates, nothing would get lost.

Secure Pac is a company that delivers food and toiletries for an exorbitant price paid for by family and friends. The order arrives in ten days, and the inmate picks it up at the distributing center. If the guard has an attitude, the order is late. No guards are made accountable for any losses. Correct the problem? Why? They're only inmates.

When an inmate is transferred to another facility before his or her commissary order arrives and is "lost en route" and the inmate inquires about the said order, the DOC tells him or her that the inmate gave the commissary order to another inmate before leaving. A $100 order? I think not. What is the inmate's recourse? None. No guards are made accountable for these losses.

I never understood why inspections of any business—and prison is a business—are announced ahead of time. It doesn't make sense in any business. It only gives the facility time to clean things up. Inspections should be spontaneous, so everything is transparent, not swept under the carpet. DOC, in fact, all government, doesn't want transparency. They all have something to hide.

At an Arizona prison at inspection time, everything was spic-and-span. The facility and the kitchen was clean, and the food was edible. What a treat for the inmates. Of course it was a dog-and-pony show. What a farce. The system is odious at best.

I'm not advocating sending out for Chinese food every day, but it should be satisfactory, at least a five on the scale of one to ten.

CHAPTER 9

HEALTH CARE, DEATH CARE

This is a pathetically sad chapter. The words *health care* in the prison system is a misnomer at best and criminal at worst, as you will read in this chapter.

If you believe what the DOC website tells you about health care, you are surely delusional. In one state, inmates pay $100 per year for medical care. Federal prisons require a $2 to $8 copay. If an inmate is indigent, he or she doesn't have to pay anything. But as we shall see, indigent or not, the health care is appalling. Prisons charge these fees because it discourages inmates from seeking care. And that is exactly the intention. It's a way of cutting costs, especially in private prisons where profits are the bottom line. Some prisons pay inmates who can acquire a job at four cents an hour, others thirty-four cents or a little more. It would take the inmates their whole monthly pay of $5 to see a doctor. Inmate health in the prison population is worse than the public. It is not ethical to refuse care, but they do. Dental care is only part time. After all, who needs teeth in prison?

If an inmate has a commissary account, medication is automatically deducted. Many times meds are deducted even though they weren't ordered. Who keeps the books in prison? Someone with a first-grade education? When an inmate gets a sprained ankle, he or she should at least get Tylenol or a cold pack. Only the favorite inmates get that attention. When I say favorite, I mean snitches and drug dealers. The guards know who takes or deals drugs. That's why they drug-test the inmates they know don't use. Maybe they put a druggie's name on the container. It sounds plausible to me.

The nurses and doctors who work for the prison are more likely to have been absent from the larger hospital care system, especially in for-profit private prisons. The doctors and nurses who work in the prisons like the hours. There isn't usually anyone in the hospital ward at night. It's usually on call. The overall health care lacks apathy, experience, and empathy. In my opinion, nurses who work in the prison system can't cut it in a hospital environment. They wouldn't get away with reusing bloody gloves on a second or third person or using one syringe in different vials. They would just be unceremoniously let go. Large hospitals don't want bad publicity either.

One amazingly cruel account is of a forty-eight-year-old woman who was on suicide watch and put in a cage outside in the sun for what was to be only ten minutes but turned out to be four hours. A nonviolent offender who pleaded for water was ignored! She had second-degree burns and organ failure before some idiot finally realized (probably after his nap) that this poor soul was still out in the sun. No one was prosecuted for her death. I'm sure the death certificate read "died of natural causes" while sunbathing in a cage. Someone put her in that cage and was responsible for letting her out. Criminal? Yes! Inhumane? Yes! But not in the DOC system.

That's only one pathetic example of how humans are treated and the tragedies I will write about. Inmates are subhuman and treated worse than dogs. Would you treat your dog like that? How can the guards who perpetrate these heinous and odious acts live with themselves and go home to their families? It's rhetorical.

In another case, a female inmate was wrongly diagnosed as having arthritis, a tragic misdiagnosis. She died in prison of bone cancer instead. I would give the doctor who diagnosed her an F and a pink slip. Back to school, you imbecile! I swear the doctors and nurses in the prison infirmary were at the bottom of the graduation list, finishing last!

I have to interrupt here. I just read an article that a medical worker an Ohio prison said that "working for the prison was fun." Fun! Did she think she was working at a county fair?

A female inmate patient in a wheelchair with a kidney dialysis complained for months that she was bleeding from her port. She died because her hemodialysis stunt had ruptured. The official cause was "death of natural causes." Do you see the pattern?

According to DOC regulations, first responders are trained in basic life support. They will respond to provide care within three minutes of an emergency. Now, does a guard have the perception to differentiate an emergency? Do they have the training? So let us say they do. Where were the first responders when Mr. M bled to death? One prison guard said he was afraid to act. Morons! You try to stop the bleeding and call first responders, who by the way do not respond in three minutes. That's another DOC lie. Where was the training for these five hopeless, helpless, heartless guards while they stood around and let a human being die without helping? It doesn't take a first responder to help someone who is bleeding. Apply pressure to the wound, period. Now do you understand when I said in a previous chapter that there is no training, especially in a for-profit prison. A monkey could apply pressure to a wound. It's despicable.

A man in a southern prison pleaded for help while having a heart attack. Where were the three-minute responders? Again it's rhetorical. The man died.

The public should know that these horrific acts happen in prison. The DOC certainly doesn't advertise these deaths on the website. All you see is "natural causes." You're not going to get the truth even if you hound them. You need an F. Lee Bailey on your side.

When an inmate was suffering a heart attack, another inmate stepped in to give him CPR. The result was discipline for the inmate who had the audacity to try to save a fellow inmate. A guard stood by and refused to call for medical help. Why? Why didn't he call for first responders or apply CPR himself? The guard would rather punish an inmate who was trying to do the right thing.

Gang members beat another inmate to death. There's no surprise there. The man was serving time for bad checks. In 2016, a forty-five-year-old inmate at a northern prison facility died because he was given the wrong medication. I will bet the reason on the death certificate read "death by natural causes."

Medical syringes are reused over and over again without changing needles. Is it incompetence or apathetic? Either way, it saves money, which is good for the profit margin. For-profit prisons will make their money and cut corners any way they can get away with. It reminds me of WW2 concentration camps using prisoners until they die, something to be discarded.

One out of ten inmates have AIDS, the same number for hep C, not counting other health issues and illnesses from unsanitary conditions.

Female prison guards and guards' wives have sex with inmates for $500 or even less, especially in high-profile prisons. How hygienic is that? You know it's true. We all know that rape is rampant in prisons, no matter if it's a male or female facility. But if you want the opposite sex, you pay. Everyone turns the other way.

Arizona has a homicide rate of 25 percent, higher than the national average. More often than not, inmates suffer serious preventable injuries, disfigurements, and deaths according to one federal agency.

An inmate brought a lawsuit against DOC because he was denied treatment for two years for a growth on his penis. It was cancer, and his penis was amputated, but not before it spread to his stomach. Could his death have been preventable if he had received treatment right away? It's quite possible, but who cares? He's just a number.

A couple of inmates were sitting outside of the medical facility when another inmate came up to them, took out his private part, urinated in a cup, took a sip, and threw the rest away. It was the same cup that inmates drank out of at chow!

There are human rights violations perpetrated every day in all prisons in America. Most are not accounted for. Dead people don't talk. We're a supposedly civilized country, but not anymore. America the Beautiful? America the Ugly. There is very little treatment or none at all in the penal system for drug abuse or any other rehabilitation. DOC says there is, but you judge. If you ask a former inmate, he or she will tell you the truth.

There are many senseless deaths in prisons all over America. The courts, DOC, and wardens should be held accountable, not sweep every incident under the rug. Fix the system! Inmates are beaten to death, gang-raped, and murdered by other inmates, even in a nonviolent minimum-security cell block. From what I've been told and read, most of the violence occurs in the showers and bathrooms. Why isn't there a permanent guard in these areas? Oh, never mind. The guard would just get paid to look the other way.

The guards know who the offenders are. They know who has cell phones and who uses drugs because the guards bring them in. Ask anyone who's been incarcerated. The prisons are infested with drugs. How could an inmate possibly get clean or rehabilitated?

That's why the guards say to inmates, "You'll be back." Another bed is filled. That's why I call DOC the "Department of Corruption."

Suicides are classified as natural causes and reported as such. Why aren't all deaths in prison autopsied? Why are many deaths reported as an unknown cause? Find out! If I had an inmate who died while incarcerated, I would sure as hell have an autopsy and promptly. If foul play were found, DOC would have a lawsuit on their hands. That's why. How can a healthy inmate with no known health problems be classified as "death unknown"? Try using that excuse in the private sector.

Many bodies are not claimed and buried on prison grounds. According to the *Arizona Republic*, there were 470 attempts of self-harm and suicides in an eleven-month period in a western incarcerated system. Mentally ill inmates often have their medication withheld, leading to suicides. Why? Because of incompetence and because they can. The fact is that health care (and I use the term loosely) in prisons all over America are cut, especially in private prisons.

Inmates are denied emergency care or care in a timely manner, as I have written in this chapter. Inmates are denied their insulin and medications. I have to ask again: Where is the humanity? It's left on the other side of the barbwire fence.

There is often no immunization for HIV or hep C. Unknown bleeding goes unattended. Many private prisons have no one attending at night. Doctors or nurses must be called in. Now that's an inconvenience. The guards are reluctant to call one.

One for-profit health-care provider, a private company that serves prisons, deflected responsibility for insulin contamination. In a southern prison, an inmate attempted suicide in 2012 after not receiving his psychotropic medication for an entire month. According to DOC, the medical company who serviced the prison was found noncompliant. The inmate was found hanging by a bedsheet in his cell. The company had a contract servicing for-profit prisons for three years, effective June 2012 for $349 million. In less than four months, the company made a major mistake. One of their nurses, whom the Board of Nurses was already investigating for undisclosed reasons, used the same needle in a second vial and then put the vial of insulin in the refrigerator with other vials of insulin and used it on 103 other inmates. The medical company did not notify county officials until eight days later.

In such close living conditions, rape, sexual activity, HIV, hep C, contagious diseases, parasites in the water, and meat that the US Department of Agriculture called rancid and served to inmates are all recipes for disaster. A female inmate with a history of breast cancer was denied her medication. Another female inmate with a golf-sized lump was denied care. What do you think their chances of survival were? That's rhetorical.

Many inmates are punished for complaining and called disrespectful when questioning their medications or diagnosis. On the outside, people are encouraged to question their care, especially on medication. Doctors and nurses are not infallible.

One inmate was disciplined for asking a nurse to change her bloody glove before examining him. That should be a no-brainer to any layperson, never mind a medical professional. See a pattern. It's apathetic or just plain stupid. Inmates, like I said, are treated like animals, less than human with no feelings or souls. They're like trash that can be easily disposed of with no questions asked.

In 2012, another health provider nurse in a women's complex gave a woman her medication by having the inmate lick the powered medication from her hand. That is treating an inmate like an animal. It's subhuman and inane.

If guards or officers want respect, like everyone else inside or outside the fence, they have to earn it. It's not a given. And from what I've seen over the years at visitation and calling DOC, they have not earned my respect.

According to the DOC website manual 1101.12, if an inmate is on a hunger strike, the staff will confiscate all the inmate's food. The inmate will not be able to purchase food while on hunger strike. Why deprive an inmate of food when he or she will end the hunger strike when he or she is ready? I know DOC has their own reasoning, but sometimes they don't make sense to the layperson.

According to 31.2.3.1, seriously ill inmates are placed in isolation. Upon release from isolation, there is a follow-up mental health evaluation. According to 1101.08, DOC will make every effort to maintain the inmate's life while in the prison complex. And according to 1.3, all staff are obligated to engage in lifesaving measures regardless of cause. As you've read earlier, that is not always the case. Really! If you believe that, I have a bridge for sale in the Arabian Desert.

All the DOC manual is for them to cover their backsides and fool the public. But you can't fool someone who has had an inmate in the system. We know the truth. A justice professor at a prominent college said, "When the state locks someone up, they assume responsibility to provide safe and humane conditions."

An ADC newsletter issued in 2012 listed written care notifications to a medical provider for contract violations, including inadequate staffing level, a decrease in routine care, incorrect or incomplete prescriptions and refill procedures, inconsistent medical documentation, lack of responsiveness to incidents urgency discrepancies, lack of reporting requirements, and unresponsive approach to inmates' grievances. ADC blamed this medical facility, and they in turn blamed ADC. Someone should have checked the background before hiring this company, which has a history of abuse and neglect. ADC terminated the contract and replaced it with another, basically another profit contractor for another. There is no reason to think anything will change. Medical staff in private for-profit prisons are discouraged from dispensing anything but ibuprofen.

In the West under a certain governor's watch, the suicide rate has increased. Look it up. Drug overdoses, homicides, untreated medical conditions, and incompetent guards are also the cause for inmates' deaths. Most are cataloged as unknown or natural causes. Is everyone in prison a hundred years old? A nineteen-year-old dies of natural causes. That should put a red flag up! An inmate is found bloody and beaten to death, but the cause is unknown.

An in-house investigation is worthless. Everyone knows DOC does nothing but cover up. It's business as usual. According to a former deputy warden, the lack of full disclosure of an inmate's deaths is intentional. The cover-up starts as soon as the incident is reported, omitting flag words, eliminating relevant individuals, and cutting back on witness lists. By the time the report is written up, it's clean and sterile: "cause of death natural or unknown."

CHAPTER 10

THE CORRUPT LEGAL SYSTEM

Why vote? In this case, the judge was a big deal in a small town. Many organizations are supposed to check the DOC system to make sure the prison and justice run honestly and correctly. Do these organizations do any good? I see no improvement so far.

As I've said, the odds rest with the prosecutors. The verdict comes from the top down. The judges, the prosecutors, and the lawyers lie, and we all know that the police lie. What chance does a defendant have in a justice system like ours? Our justice system is supposed to be a civil system. As anyone in their right mind knows, the police lie to get a conviction. A common ploy is to stop you and say you have rear light out (which you don't). Then they check your breath for alcohol as well as the inside of your vehicle. This is the real world and not "a blue-blood police show."

They must have probable cause to search your vehicle, and they will find it if they have to make one up. I have known decent, honest police in my life, but that was in my home city in the 1960s and 1970s. They looked out for me when I owned a business at that time. They would come around in the evening when it was dark out and I had to work late by myself to check on me to see if I was okay. I was ever so grateful to them. That was the time of the cop walking on the street beat.

Now the police are out of control. If they are so afraid of the work, then they are in the wrong business. And why shoot to kill, especially in cases of the mentally ill? Why not shoot in the leg or shoulder? I'm guessing that shooting to kill would eliminate a witness, especially one on one with no one around. Why excess force? Why twenty to thirty shots toward a person sitting in a vehicle? Is it overkill? Or does every cop have to have target practice?

Just like the medical profession, the police department has a code of silence. That's why in both professions people die for no reason. What about the chokehold that police and prison officers use? Many times multiple police officers or prison guards are beating on one suspect; often the suspect has their hands cuffed and is being kicked and punched by multiple officers.

It's chicken shit to me. Is that necessary? It reminds me of a gang bang. These officers act like animals. What harm can a person do with his or her hands cuffed? The police say it's justified because they called them names. Are they two years old? If your skin is so thin that a name offends you, again you're in the wrong business. Isn't that freedom of speech, our constitutional right? Or is being spit on a reason to beat someone to death? Some officers are so insecure that the only way to feel good about themselves is by brutality. Where is our humanity in this country? It's been lost in corruption!

Texan taxpayers paid $900 million in 2017 to hold people awaiting trial. Reformers want to release low-risk and nonviolent offenders with pretrial supervision. They can't do that because bail bondsmen won't make money. They are leading the opposition. Louisiana, Mississippi, Alabama, Oklahoma, Texas, and Arizona are the top-six states that send more people to prison. It's a political choice. There's that P-word again, political.

The public is assured or assumes that officials are honest and have at least the minimal amount of intelligence and then justice will prevail … until it's their turn to face the judicial system. The system is flawed, as are officials. If evidence is overlooked, no one will admit it. That would make someone look incompetent, and that's not good for your job.

A private-run prison in the South was closed in 2012 for what someone called a "horror scene." This prison was effectually run by gangs and corrupt guards, a brutal and lawless prison. A month after the close-down of this facility, the Justice Department announced it would phase out private prisons.

DOC said it shut down the prison "not because of unrestrained violence, but because of budget cuts." Private prisons don't lose money. This facility was run by a corporation that is among one of the largest in the nation. Some of the guards themselves were gang members who would let inmates out of their cells to assault other unsuspecting rivals. Gladiator-style fights were organized by guards who would bet on the outcome. Marijuana odor was so heavy that it was like walking into a club. At one time, the town mayor was also the prison warden. Is that a conflict of interest?

The law states that a person is presumed innocent until proven guilty, but not in this country and particularly not in many states. The prosecutors determine the accused guilt even before going to court. You are assumed guilty, and you have to prove your innocence. Most prosecutors aren't interested in the truth, only a conviction, unless you have lots of assets or if you are a politician or celebrity like Claus von Bulow or Vince Neil, who once spent fifteen days in jail for his friend's manslaughter. How about Richard James Herrin who admitted killing his girlfriend with a hammer in 1977? The list goes on. Justice is surely blind, deaf, and dumb.

Murderers get off, and the poor bastard who gets caught with a bong in a vehicle goes to prison for two years. Before this new law President Obama passed, getting caught with over an ounce or two received eight to forty-five years in prison. Really! Marijuana? When I was a teen, my father always said that lawyers are shysters. He never explained why he thought that way. Decades later I found out.

I don't know why my father held on to that opinion because he never had a brush with the law. His only interaction with lawyers was on business advice for his properties and his will. That moniker stuck with me to this day.

I don't mind lawyers making money, but bleeding people dry is just plain greed. I know of only one lawyer in my entire long life whom I trusted, and I took his free advice. That was a lawyer in Pampa, Texas. I thank him for his honest and sound advice. You know who you are.

Are the US courts fair? Hell no. Not even close. I don't believe that court-appointed lawyers or public defenders work diligently for a client. First, they have overloaded cases, and second, they don't get paid the big money. In the case of one inmate's appeal, the court-appointed lawyer's father had to get certain files and other information for her because she was too busy to retrieve them.

Do you think a public defender would try their best to defend an indigent client? I think not. In fact, I know not. This inmate's lawyer didn't object to any of the false statements the arresting police told. She answered the judge either yes or no, period. She never questioned why the prosecutor did not have the transcript of the statement the inmate made; nor did she have the file before going to court. That's a piss-poor lawyer in my book. The judge asked where the transcript was, and the prosecutor said he couldn't find it.

The defendant's lawyer raised no objection. The judge should have adjourned the court so the prosecutor could go and retrieve them. After all, he was a prosecutor for years, and to make a mistake like this is unconscionable and detrimental to any inmate's case. That's why I say the case was decided before it was taken to court. The judge probably went to lunch with the police and the prosecutor. After all they were all from the same town. The judge ran consecutively with no opposition for years. What does that say about the judicial system in that town? The judge has carte blanche.

Even if someone is not guilty, the person may plead guilty and take a plea bargain because the person figures he or she will get railroaded anyway, so a plea will get him or her a shorter sentence. It's better than ten to twenty years for something the person didn't do, Remember, the police and prosecutor have the advantage unless you are loaded. If you don't have any money for your defense, you're screwed! That's not justice. That's a kangaroo court.

A court-appointed lawyer is like a judge advocate general (JAG) lawyer for the military. You will never get a fair trial because the JAG works for the general and does what the general says. Look at what the acronym means. The TV show *JAG* will fight for his client, but that's just in the movies, of course. Who has the clout, you or the general?

A police officer can lie when someone is giving a statement or being interrogated. Can you lie to protect yourself? Hell no! When arrested, keep your mouth shut. Let the court prove your guilt. Don't say a word because even the most innocent of statements will be turned against you. Lawyer up. It is the prosecutor's job to find evidence against you, not the other way around. It's not your job to incriminate yourself. Many times a person isn't given their Miranda rights. The police say they do. So who's going to believe you? I'm not advocating committing a crime, but there may be circumstantial evidence that can play in your sentencing. Know your rights. Strange bedfellows are judges, DAs, appointed lawyers, and police.

Never take your case to a lone judge. A panel of twelve gives you a better shot. I would go with twelve of my peers rather than one lone judge who doesn't have a clue about the life of the man on the street. At least the twelve jurors don't have a link to the prosecutors or the lawyers.

A person has a better chance of a plea bargain than going to court. When your case is taken to court, it takes time and money from the state. You will pay dearly for that. Like I said before, most judges favor the prosecutors and police. It goes with the territory. Protect the public, my ass. Protect their own.

There's the story about a police officer stopping a vehicle for having the rear light out. That one is so lame. But the public falls for it. It's just a ruse to smell a person's breath or look in the person's car for anything they could use against him or her. I would call that "illegal smell and look."

Many years ago in my hometown back east, a policeman would stop women for some trumped-up infraction, have her follow him to a secluded area, and then rape her. This one particular case always haunted me. She was found on the highway where the cop dropped her off, naked in the middle of a snowy winter. She wasn't the first case. Many women back then wouldn't report it because they were ashamed. I was always frightened to drive alone at night because of that one rotten apple in the barrel. It's a true story!

When I was growing up, the police would walk the beat in my city. They were helpful and friendly. They didn't treat everyone like criminals. These days when you see police, you automatically think, *What did I do wrong?* You know you didn't, and I'm in my seventies. Now if you approach a police officer, he or she is liable to shoot you if you have a candy bar in your hands and then plant a gun or drugs on you.

Why do police have to shoot to kill or use a taser gun to subdue? Gangsters shoot their victims in the knees. Why can't police use the same strategy? That would stop anyone in their tracks. They shoot to kill and leave no witnesses. In one case, one police officer beat up a man while three other cops looked on. Protect and serve? I think not.

A cop in the Midwest in the 1960s was as crooked as they come. This cop had no credentials. His résumé was all made up. No one checked. He falsified his military discharge, saying he was honorably discharged when in fact he was AWOL twice with no honorable discharge. He had a not so clean record. It is an abomination that not one of the jobs he applied for checked his references.

After a while, he became an undercover cop. He had hundreds put in prison by making up false stories and planting false evidence when there was none at all. He even planted heroin on someone when there was no heroin in his city at the time. Marijuana yes, but no hard stuff.

This cop wanted to make a name for himself because he could. There were signs of inconsistencies throughout his police career, but no one, not the police chief or the mayor, thought or bothered to check. No one brought up these suspicions. He never had a witness to his arrests, although it was police policy that two police officers be present at an arrest. There's that code of silence again.

And he counted on it. If someone did get suspicious, he would move to another county. The population of these towns never questioned him either. They thought he was cleaning up the city to make it safe for the residents. On many of the arrests, he had never met the person or set eyes on him before. The person was in the wrong place at the wrong time. He had only known some of the names of the persons he arrested and others not. All the arrests were bogus. Over seven hundred people went to prison on his word alone in a ten-year period.

A policeman's word is honest, right? It's not to be questioned. He didn't use his county's crime lab for testing, which was unusual, but again no one questioned him. He used a big city lab for drug testing because he knew someone at that lab. He could sneak drugs out to plant on potential victims or in their homes or vehicles. Heck, he was doing a good job getting the drug "scum" off the street, right?

One day a seasoned undercover cop at one of his new counties was suspicious because no one ever saw him in action. This other undercover cop had made two, maybe three, drug arrests in the whole time he was in this particular town, and it was only marijuana. This new hotshot made three heroin arrests on his first day. It was too good to be true. His fellow cop set a trap for him. This time he was arrested on a lesser charge, but nothing to do with the false arrests. He could go on to another state and do his harm again.

As you have read, prison corruption comes in a variety of ways, from smuggling in contraband, engaging in sexual favors, and smuggling in weapons and cell phones, to name a few. We must not leave out guards facilitating prison breaks. Can these activities be curtailed? Yes, but it must come from the top down.

This concludes the chapter on prison corruption. If you think it can't happen to you, think again. The oxymorons are "truth in justice" and "Department of Correction." Lady Liberty is blind. Why do you think she wears a blindfold?

 CHAPTER 11

THREE STRIKES

Politicians will say and do anything to get elected. You don't have to go back very far in time to realize that. Not many politicians keep their word. With the old three-strikes law that President Clinton enacted, people would get life in prison without parole for three federal offenses.

Why not rehabilitate? That won't get a politician elected. You have to put fear into the public and have them think they will be safer with tougher laws. Anyone can learn not to use the five-finger discount. A parent can teach a child not to steal, so why not the justice system? After all, it's called the "Department of Correction," isn't it?

So correct! An inmate serving twenty-five years for a nonviolent crime is a crime. Let the punishment fit the crime and not just hand out sentences willy-nilly. I know my words will not go over well with a lot of readers, but just think of it for a moment. I'm not a bleeding heart. I just think that the system is more interested in placating the public, which I may add does not have a clue on how the system works or how cruel and archaic it is. This is the twenty-first century after all. Other civilized countries recognize this, so why not America?

America represents 5 percent of the world. But we hold 25 percent of the world's prison population. Now I'm saying civilized countries here, not countries that throw stones at a woman until she's dead.

 **CHAPTER 12**

GUARDS AND OFFICERS WITH BENEFITS

This chapter is dedicated to all inmates who have been mistreated, abused, and murdered in the penal system by apathetic guards and officers. The prisons are a breeding ground for hate and enmity propagated by sadistic guards and officers. Not all, but most after a while. It becomes natural to be a bully, truculent, and disdainful. When have you ever heard a guard say "I love my job because I want to help the inmates"? They are guards because they have no other career options and want to wield power over the powerless as well as life and death.

Do the guards get psychological testing before being hired? Or are they just thugs in uniform? DOC says they get tested. But ADC says a lot of things that are not true. From what I've read, there's not intensive testing. All prison personnel should have at least one year intensive testing. What training do the guards and officers really receive besides on-the-job in graft, bullying, extortion, bribery, stealing, lying, harassing, and, last but not least, beating and killing? Am I exaggerating? No! Ask anyone who has been in any prison or jail in America. Is everyone out to lunch or on a donut run when training is in session? I know this will upset many prison personnel, but it's the truth.

If you don't have hate in your heart when you enter prison, you may very well when you are released. Prisons are a breeding ground for duplicity, machinations, and nefarious and obstructive behavior. And that's only the guards. Doesn't anyone wonder about all the drugs and phones that are certainly contraband? For example, look at guards ordering hits on inmates to protect their associations with gangs. In one prison back east, a guard was paid thousands of dollars to pick up drugs and cell phones and bring them into the prison. He was eventually caught and sent to prison. Drugs and cell phones are a priority, as are cigarettes a smuggling business in the prison. And it is a business.

Two guards forced a mentally ill inmate into a scalding shower as a form of punishment. He died of his wounds. Guards also give favors to inmates to take out prisoners. Sexual favors are also rampant in all prisons. I've heard of guards' wives being snuck into a prison to pleasure an inmate, for a fee of course. It's $500 for two minutes or maybe less.

I think these few examples tell all about corrupt guards. There are more of the same stories in all the prisons in America. The saying goes that anybody can be bought. I don't want to sound too cynical. What happened to our humanity? Are we as Americans so desensitized that cruel and inhumane actions don't bother us? Wherever there is money to be made, there is corruption. I won't say that all people in this chapter are narcissists. I would say that more than not, they are duplicitous, imperious, and prone to derision. Remember, power corrupts!

Many guards and officers should be incarcerated themselves, but the old-boy system protects them. When you are in power, you can get away with anything, even murder. What would you call it when two guards hold a mentally ill inmate under a scalding shower? The inmate later died of his wounds. That, to me, is murder.

For example, one inmate had a work assignment working outside the fence. Someone came up to the inmate and asked him to smuggle drugs into the prison. He wouldn't, so the same day he lost his job. Why would he risk an extra five years in hell for some dope addict? Who put the dope by the fence? I'll give you one guess. The hyenas are watching the chickens.

If one out of ten nonviolent inmates in America were to be rehabilitated instead of a prison sentence, there would be fewer beds filled, many prisons would close, and the investors' bottom line would drop. Prisons are big business, period. It's bigger than any citizen could imagine. Investors are making big money out of people's misfortune.

If you ask anyone who has been in prison, he or she will tell you the truth about how the guards act. Sure, they are on good behavior on visiting day. When visitation is over, it is business as usual. How can they sleep at night? That's rhetorical. They can't have any self-respect, but they do have plenty of greed and power. But there's no conscience or character. How can they go home to their families after their shift when they act like thugs and drug pushers at work? On *Prison Talk*, an officer defended the guards, saying, "There are only a few that abuse their position." He must be working in a fantasy prison. That's not what I hear when I speak to ex-prisoners.

Look up *Prison Chat*. You'll get a good understanding about how the prison system works. The people who write on *Prison Chat* don't make things up. They tell it like it is. They are speaking for their loved ones who can't. Retaliation is rampant in prison. Families are concerned and apprehensive about abuse from guards and other inmates. Harassment goes on every single day from the guards.

For example, one inmate was sleeping soundly when a female guard went by his bed and banged on his bunk to wake him up. Why? Because she could, period. Another inmate had two sixteen-ounce plastic bottles of water he was using for weightlifting. A guard came along and confiscated them. I guess the guard was thirsty.

When something is confiscated, the guard must give the inmate a receipt. That is a rule most guards ignore. What is the recourse? None. With no receipt given to the inmate, he or she has no proof. It's the inmate's word against the guard. The guards take what they want. All they have to say is that the item is contraband. But an inmate who purchases fifteen bottles of water and resells the water to other inmates for profit is okay because he or she is one of them.

Do you think the guards bring in contraband for nothing? They are making money while potentially getting an inmate an extra five years added to their sentence. Who's going to turn in a guard to the proper authorities and take a chance at getting killed? The other guards look the other way. Hey, it's money under the table, a perk, if you will. Every person working in a prison should be searched, period. They should also be tested for drugs from an outside company. Are they above the law? Are they to be trusted more than the inmates?

Pepto-Bismol must be expensive in the prison commissary. Barbara's inmate had a bottle partly used, and a guard confiscated it and told the inmate it was contraband. What? It was purchased at the prison commissary. Barbara ordered a book from an approved book company. The name of the book was *Beautiful Outlaw,* a book about Jesus. The book was confiscated as contraband.

The officer told Barbara's inmate that rather than sending the book back to the company, he could instead "donate the book" to the prison library. What kind of double standard is that? I can see no consistency in the DOC system whatsoever. It all works on a whim.

Where is the big C in Department of Correction? No, really? Where? I have read every page of the DOC website anybody can, and as far as I can deduce, the website is all propaganda to fool the public. Many inmates keep their nose clean, but the guards lie and play games with the inmates.

I won't say that all guards and officers are complicit. A female guard said that all negative things she's read on websites aren't true. She was a newbie. Oh, she'll make a great guard. Or the other guards will eat her up and spit her out.

In prison, an inmate must keep their area clean and orderly. One day a guard went into Barbara's inmate's cell and swept everything off the shelf onto the floor. His excuse was that he was looking for drugs. As I've said before, the guards know who does and doesn't use. Otherwise who would they sell drugs to?

Barbara's inmate told the guard, "You better put everything back where it was."

The guard cleaned up the mess he made.

In 1870, two wardens started the National Prison Association Conference to focus on rehabilitation. In 1971 the association was renamed. Now the conference focuses on selling tear gas, stun guns, leg irons, tasers, ankle bracelets, and prison furniture. It's big business again. We're going backward, people!

Graft

In the dictionary, graft is defined as corruption. It is a behavior of dishonesty or unethical conduct of a person of authority. It is a specific type of political corruption for personal gain.

 CHAPTER 13

ERRATIC SENTENCING

Barbara's inmate received eight years for carrying marijuana. He had no weapons, and he was nonviolent. Not every sentence is equal or fair. It may depend on the state, prosecutor, or judge.

A North Carolina woman was sentenced to twenty-five to thirty years for bludgeoning her husband to death. One of the largest cocaine traffickers in history received thirty-five years for distributing four hundred tons annually, backed by the lethal drug cartel and five terrorist groups.

A police chief in the South directed his officers to frame people on different offenses because of pressure from community leaders. He ruined hundreds of lives for false convictions. He received a whopping three years in prison. In 2016, an athlete from the South received six years for shooting his girlfriend to death. Wouldn't it have been easier to just separate?

In Cincinnati, a man murdered his wife and received life in prison. He is eligible for parole in twenty years. In 2004 an actor was arrested in Kentucky for possession of seventeen grams of marijuana and two controlled drugs. He received a one-year suspended sentence. Someone else of lesser importance would have received at least five to eight years.

A few years ago, a man killed another with a bullet in the head; he received twenty years and was released in five. What's wrong with this picture? A $150 shoplifting spree and an unarmed burglary landed a man in prison for fifty years to life. A doctor received six years for drugging a woman patient and got out in four. This same doctor raped his stepdaughter.

A drug dealer received five years for murdering a drug buyer. A man got fifteen years for murdering another man. He was out in five and killed again. Many nonviolent convictions will get you sixteen years to life. In 2017, a woman in a western state received five years in federal prison for killing her child. Inconsistency? Is that the correct vernacular?

Five states have a requirement of 50 percent of a sentence served. Three states require 100 percent of the sentence served. The rest of the states require mostly 85 percent of the sentence served. The New Mexico website says they will allow veterans charged with crimes, I assume nonviolent, to choose treatment instead of prison. The Veterans Court has a 7.1 percent repeat offenders rate; the rest of the country is at 43 percent. Now doesn't that show that rehabilitation works? I'm impressed.

I lived in Italy for a total of ten years and always felt safe. There are no mass shootings in Italy because of the strict gun laws and the Italian mentality. Now there are pickpockets galore, but they are not in the same category, are they? And they are not violent. You wouldn't know it if they picked your pocket or backpack anyway. It's an art.

The United States has the highest number of mass shootings compared to other civilized countries. One president has made it easier, not harder, for mentally ill persons to purchase guns. Could someone explain to me why a deer or bird hunter needs a scope, silencer, RIP bullets (the deadliest ammo on earth), and a high-powered rifle? That's rhetorical. It's overkill. That's not sporting. Who needs an automatic or machine gun? Only the killers do.

For decades, the less the sheriffs spend on food for inmates, the more money they pocket. A former sheriff was jailed for feeding inmates corn dogs and pocketing $2 million. Inmates are fed low-carb diets and donated food, and sheriffs get large profits from jailhouse kitchens. A Monroe sheriff pocketed $110,459 over three years. That's a lot of money in the South.

In a southern city, a prison correction chief was sentenced to twenty years for running the longest and largest graft in history. The prosecutor recommended thirteen years. A police commissioner was charged with accepting thousands of dollars and gifts. He was given a $221,000 fine and no jail time. And during his nomination to head a political office, he was charged with lying to the Bush administration and sentenced to four years. He was out in three and received three years of home confinement. That was eight felony charges, including false statements.

At his trial, he said he was very disappointed in the prosecutors and the judge. Aren't we all? Even he agrees that the system is corrupt. He also said that federal prosecutors hit low-level nonviolent offenders with conspiracy counts that carry more prison time and some inmates get life for nonviolent crimes. He obviously saw the reality of corruption.

Governor P. is a hypocrite on opioids. He declared an emergency to address the opioid epidemic but accepted money from an opioid maker. Six executives have been indicted for illegal kickbacks to doctors who improperly handed out prescriptions for the drug. They were bribing doctors to prescribe this addictive drug. Shame on the doctors who took an oath to do no harm. Meanwhile, this company gave $5 million to antimarijuana legislation. It's corrupt!

A former deputy's son was charged with sexual assault and kidnapping. He was lucky enough to go to a mental institute and not prison. What about the other mentally ill who are in prison and being abused? His records are sealed, only because his parent was a deputy.

Two judges in Tampa sentenced juveniles to private youth detention centers run by Tampa Child Care. These two judges received $2.6 million in kickbacks. The youths did not have lawyers present. It was a revolving-door court, with the proceedings lasting a minute or two. They were sentenced instead of given probation. The high court is looking into whether thousands of these cases should be overturned. These juveniles were charged with stealing loose change from a car, writing a prank joke, or possessing drug paraphernalia. I spoke about the bong in an earlier chapter.

For many of these kids, it was their first offense. The judges received more than seven years in prison with their plea agreement. Will they appeal? Hell yes. Will they get released early? I have no doubt they will.

 CHAPTER 14

FOR-PROFIT PRIVATE PRISONS: A DISGRACE TO AMERICA'S CIVILITY

A private prison corporate lobbyist wrote the War on Drugs hysteria. Police and prison guard unions are among the largest contributors to politicians. One private for-profit company has a million beds worldwide. It's a lucrative business indeed. What is a private prison's incentive to rehabilitate? None.

I've had years to research the US prison system. As far as I can see and research, they are all corrupt in some form or another. Before I did, I had no idea that there was such a thing as for-profit prisons. I have come to believe that they are a scourge on our society.

For this chapter, I will mainly concentrate on private prisons. The largest private prison company in America runs sixty-six private prisons, specifically ninety-one thousand beds across twenty states. They contributed $1.7 million in political contributions in the past ten years. In 2012, they proposed an offer to purchase and upgrade the federal prison system in forty-eight states. The company wanted a twenty-year contract and a guarantee of 90 percent bed occupancy rate.

Do you think these corporations get the beds filled legally? They need the help of the courts, governors, and judges. Another group operates three major private prisons and is publicly traded. It is the second-largest profit prison group, which brought in $1.6 billion in 2011. They own sixty-five private prisons and 65,700 beds across the country. The group paid a lobbyist $2.5 million and made $2.9 million in political contributions.

The only thing that matters is the bottom line for the shareholders and millions of dollars in pay to the apathetic CEOs. Executive pay for one of these companies in 2011 was $3.7 million. For lobbyists in a ten-year period, it was $17 million. The shareholders should be ashamed of themselves for their auspicious investment.

Americans treat our animals better than inmates. Our pets get better food. If someone mistreats an animal, that person gets jail time. A prison mistreats an inmate, and everyone looks the other way.

Politics is the bane of America's existence. It corrupts everything it's in contact with. Some contractors in certain states require 100 percent occupancy. Otherwise the state will have to pay the corporations for each empty bed. Where do they get the inmates to fill the beds? They incarcerate the young, the mentally ill, and the inmates with no money for a fair trial who have to use an incompetent public attorney.

If you send a person to a federal prison for a nonviolent crime, that individual could very well end up radicalized. Now you go from an offense like a one-time DWI or marijuana charge to a jihadist.

Someone on painkillers is in an accident or stopped. That person gets a DWI, goes to prison, and loses his or her job and family. If anyone thinks it can't happen to them because they aren't criminals, check out the Arizona Justice Project. People who haven't done anything wrong think the justice system will rule in their favor. Now add a zealous prosecutor who is bound to get a conviction and bang! Guilty! A child lies about an innocent adult touching them inappropriately, and again, guilty! The person goes to prison and is registered as a sex offender for life.

We are not a democracy in America. We are not all equal in the eyes of the judicial system. The prosecutors won't look at new evidence because they don't want to look inept. A governor in the Northeast had a policy that wouldn't consider appeals because as a woman, she didn't want to look weak on crime. That's a politician for you. They care more about their political interests before public welfare. The judicial system doesn't care if you are innocent or not. You're in custody, and they will get a conviction. It happens to people more often than you know. Like I said, arrest could happen to anyone. Remember, beds have to be filled. Anyone who thinks that putting someone away for a nonviolent crime without any rehabilitation will make the public safe is delusional.

Private prisons are built to make money. What does that say about the system? It's money for the investors. These corporations have subcompanies and sub-subcompanies. It's a paper chase to find all the investors and CEOs. A large corporation management was replaced with another ill-equipped company because they failed to control a riot and had a culture of disorganization, disengagement, and disregard of policies. In 2010, there were 8.2 million marijuana arrests. Eighty-eight percent of all arrests combined were for nonviolent marijuana-related offenses. The key word here is *nonviolent*.

If every nonviolent inmate were released and sent to a vocational or treatment center, many prisons would close, and politicians and investors would lose income. It is not legally wrong to invest in other people's trials and adversities, but in my book, it is morally wrong. Why not spend the money on rehab? Wouldn't that be prodigious? But as I've said, big money talks. And why should a tried-and-true method be tinkered with?

Colorado arrests have dropped significantly since the state made marijuana legal in 2014. One may legally possess one ounce of marijuana on one's person at one time. It must be kept sealed in your vehicle, must not be used in public, and can be purchased in dispensaries only. You better keep your receipt. Marijuana cannot leave the state.

When a head shop clerk sells a water pipe, he darn well knows that it will be used as a bong. But he's off the hook. I say make it illegal to sell water pipes or any other known drug paraphernalia such as bowls, vaporizers, or empty dime bags, as "they are said to be used for jewelry." Yeah, right. These are all legal to sell in head shops but not legal to possess? Now who's smoking dope? There are so many whys and no answers.

America has 5 percent of the world's population and 25 percent of the world's prisons. Europeans call the United States the "United Gulag of America." I know because I lived in Europe. As reported by *Journalism in the Public Interest*, as of 2000, there were 153 private prisons in the United States. That's twice as many people as in Communist China, which has five times our population. The United States is an incarceration nation.

Every state has an industry. California has Silicon Valley. Texas has oil. Connecticut has the insurance carriers. Massachusetts has hospitals. Arizona has a very lucrative prison system. All states have their own laws. And then there is the federal law on marijuana. So if you're into marijuana, stay within the law and guidelines, and you'll be okay. I'm not advocating for marijuana. I've never used it and never will, not even for medical reasons.

It's no secret that lobbyists work hard to supply money to political candidates. I would call that bribery. No money means no support. Wall Street institutions own two prison supply corporations. A campaign manager for a former governor in the East was also a lobbyist for one of the largest for-profit corporations.

Prison vendors have big profit investors. Commissaries are huge conglomerates with far-reaching tentacles throughout the prison system, from selling fruits to nuts. Visiting room vending machines are outrageously expensive.

Donated food is another example of saving money and getting profits up. The donated food doesn't mean the food is good for consumption. It's out-of-date or rancid. If you put enough gravy on it, no one will be the wiser, until someone gets food poisoning, that is. When you have a captive audience, it is like taking candy from a baby.

Many of these corporations are a paper chase. Some have managed everything in the prison system for over forty years. It has, as of this writing, twelve service groups. There are no names of CEOs or board of directors on any website. They have much national organizational and corporate support. Five associations support the American Jail Association and seventy other associations. The system is developed to keep names a secret, to hide who is behind all the money. I couldn't find a rehabilitation group.

One day the public may go to jail for jaywalking or spitting on the sidewalk. Bang! Beds are full, and new jails and prisons are built. You may think that I'm being facetious, but I'm not. Look at the headlines on the news: "Freedom of Speech Curtailed," or "Articles Defined as Fake News." We are becoming a society of robots, all thinking the same way. We are letting the elite rule our daily lives. If we have a different opinion, we may be called subversive, as in Russia.

The prison system is full of duplicity. It is insidious, nefarious, and out of control. Why can't we find one honest government/political official in the whole United States of 327.16 million people? The shareholders should be ashamed of themselves for their auspicious investments.

Politics are the bane of America's existence. It corrupts everything it's in contact with. Prison officials get kickbacks from concessions, sometimes as much as $12,000 to $30,000 a year. Is that tax-free? In Texas, inmates spent $95 million at prison commissaries in one state. When I say inmates, I mean families. Politics is a dirty business, but no more so than the Department of Corrections. Everyone has their hands in the pot.

In 2017, the attorney general wanted to make the marijuana laws tougher, even for nonviolent crimes. It makes one wonder what's in it for him. The three-strikes law did not consider rehabilitation and treatment, which would cut back on recidivism. The three-strikes law was draconian at best.

When some prisons get too crowded, the solution is to downgrade an inmate from maximum to minimum security, which means a murderer will be in a minimum-security prison. Who cares about the safety of inmates? Now if you think that your inmate is relatively safe in a minimum-security prison, think again. There were murders in Barbara's inmate's area. The online handbook doesn't mention that discrepancy. The system is very efficient in hiding the truth. If you put nonviolent inmates with violent inmates, crap happens.

In 2017, there were 1,888,772 inmates in federal prisons, costing an exorbitant $5.75 billion a year. I'm sure the inmates could be rehabbed for much less. The Bureau of Prisons says it costs over $30,000 per year for one inmate. Many families live on less. Where is the money going? In California, the cost exceeds $75,000 per inmate. It's not like they are fed steak and lobster.

If you care to know how corrupt politicians are, read *Dark Money* and *The Dark Side of Camelot*. What do these books have to do with the prison system? Everything is political! The prison system is too big to fail. In Arizona, the prison population has increased eightfold in thirty years. Anyone with a pulse can go to jail or prison—or maybe even those without a pulse as long as a bed is filled.

There are two death rows in Arizona prisons, one made up of approximately 125 inmates officially sentenced to death. The other unofficial death row reaches statewide. These are the victims of prison violence, neglect, and mistreatment. No judge condemns anyone in this group. A director of the Arizona prison system said, "There is no solitary confinement in Arizona." What is his meaning of solitary confinement? SMU is "special management units." In an intelligent person's vocabulary, SMU is solitary confinement, a type of isolation.

Amnesty International condemned Arizona's SMU and called them draconian and cruel isolation. According to the Arizona Department of Correction website, in the department order manual, department order 1.2.3.1 says inmates may be placed in isolation or in a lockdown cell. Lockdown cell is self-explanatory, but isolation in *Webster's Dictionary* means separation, keeping apart, solitariness, and seclusion. That says solitary confinement to me. An inmate cannot be held in SMU more than twenty-two hours a day and no longer than fifteen days. Do you think the DOC complies?

Many prisoners all over the United States are confined for life without human contact twenty-four hours a day. Some prisons use concrete and steel boxes. When released after spending twenty-five years in SMU, one inmate remarked that he welcomed losing his mind. Sending an inmate to SMU for more than fifteen days is cruel and inhumane punishment, according to the United Nations. I don't know why Amnesty International and the UN establish these laws if no one bothers to enforce them. If the objective is to have the inmate lose his or her sanity, the penal system is on the right track.

In the second depression of 1936, state and federal camps were set up for displaced Americans. The federal camps were sanitary. The private-owned displacement camps were horrible and filthy. This was the era of the forgotten man. Sound familiar?

 CHAPTER 15

THE SHERIFF

The voting public always amazes me. For twenty-four years, the public kept voting a notorious sheriff into office. Why? Because he used fear-mongering and overexaggerated crime. He stepped over the law line to do as he pleased in his office.

In twenty-four years, he has cost the taxpayers over $140 million in lawsuits. He's had his tax and investments redacted and purged from public records. You try that and see where it gets you. The sheriff has purchased two strip malls for $250,000, cash. In 2002, he paid $440,000 (cash) for a two-story property. All this was on a sheriff's pay and a small income from another source. When in office, bags of cash were dropped off on his office desk.

Where did the cash come from? No one knows. He refused to be audited. As a private citizen, if you try that, you land in jail. The average sheriff makes a little over $100,000 per year. That's without benefits. For someone with only a high school education, he's done well for himself in Louisiana.

During his tenure as sheriff, he's refused to prosecute more than four hundred sex offenders. In 1995, he reinstated the chain gang. He purchased a tank to show off with. It's taxpayers' money again, yet all the while he brags that he saves taxpayers money by feeding the inmates baloney sandwiches and peanut butter sandwiches. He also says that he feeds his dogs better than his inmates.

The sheriff used his power to harass and punish whistleblowers. He also used taxpayer money to investigate political rivals. He and a cohort sought grand jury indictments on a number of Supreme Court justices, budget directors, and county supervisors. This cost the county $44 million alone. The sheriff and his cohorts lost all the judgments. The two founders of a newspaper were arrested after an article was published about the grand jury investigation. All the charges were dropped against the publishers. The Louisiana County Board of Supervisors urged the publishers to sue the sheriff. They did and won $3.75 million. The sheriff had election law violations and was fined $153,000. By 2017 he had misspent over $100 million. He kept two sets of books. What happened to oversight?

The sheriff's deputies traveled to Alaska and stayed at a fishing resort. They also took trips to Disneyland. High-ranking employees were charging expensive meals and staying at luxury hotels. There was a staff party at a local amusement park.

There was also misconduct by the former sheriffs second-in-command, by the way. This person committed criminal acts, including tampering with witnesses, destroying evidence, and obstructing justice. There was no action taken against the second-in-command because the sheriff was guilty of these same acts. What a country! Supposedly we're the greatest country in the world, and the uninformed public vote in such narcissist, apathetic politicians.

On the sheriff's watch, an eighteen-year-old was locked up for four years because of a publicity stunt perpetrated by the sheriff involving a pipe bomb. A lawsuit was settled against the sheriff for $1.1 million. A detainee died in custody because she was denied medical treatment and went into a diabetic coma. The county settled this case for $3.35 million with an additional $1.8 million in legal fees. He banned cigarettes, coffee, hot lunches, and salt and pepper. Meat was off the menu. Inmates were served two meals per day.

The sheriff showed two reporters around his facility, of which we know he was very proud of. The sheriff showed the reporters the kitchen and commented on the vegetable stew with soybean products. The reporter commented that the carrots were brown and the soy looked like wood chips. The sheriff told the reporter, "It's probably dirt. Don't worry about it." Amnesty International and UCLA condemned him. What happened? No one knows.

What is wrong with our country? Why do we let people in power skirt the law and act like dictators? No one could convince the sheriff that what he was doing to the inmates was just plain wrong. This reminds me of a quote. "Never hold a discussion with a monkey when the organ grinder is in the room."

The sheriff thought he was above the law, but in 2017 he was on trial for criminal contempt. He made false statements and tried to stop further investigations against him.

And that, my friends, is the justice system in America. It's not as draconian as other countries, but it's pretty close and just as corrupt. The difference is that citizens of other Western countries call out their corrupt politicians. Americans sit back and complain. As years go by, the politicians get more corrupt because the other guy got away with it and so can they.

Printed in the United States
By Bookmasters